THE STERLING B

Hinduism

Other Books in this Series

Esther

THE STERLING BOOK OF

Hinduism

Dr Karan Singh

NEW DAWN PRESS, INC.
UK • USA • INDIA

NEW DAWN PRESS GROUP

Published by New Dawn Press Group

New Dawn Press, 2 Tintern Close, Slough, Berkshire, SL1-2TB, UK
e-mail: salesuk@newdawnpress.org

New Dawn Press, Inc., 244 South Randall Rd # 90, Elgin, IL 60123, USA
e-mail: sales@newdawnpress.com

New Dawn Press (An Imprint of Sterling Publishers (P) Ltd.)
A-59, Okhla Industrial Area, Phase-II, New Delhi-110020, INDIA
e-mail: info@sterlingpublishers.com
www.sterlingpublishers.com

The Sterling Book of: HINDUISM
© 2005, Dr Karan Singh
ISBN 1 84557 425 7
Reprint 2007

PRINTED IN INDIA

Contents

Never falter in doing your duty. God has decreed man's duty, and to fail is to disobey God. It is through duty that a man reaches perfection.
Behave with others as you would with yourself.

Publisher's Note

Sterling started this new series which focuses on the various aspects of Indian social and cultural life, be it dance, religion or philosophy. The books provide the lay readers a basic information on the subject.

The Sterling Book of Hinduism by Dr Karan Singh, an eminent scholar of Hindu philosophy, has outlined the chief facets of Hinduism as a way of life.

We have included 'Words of Wisdom' from the sacred works of Hinduism. These are excerpts taken from *Excellence in Hinduism* compiled and edited by O P Ghai.

Publication of more books on similar topics in this series is in the pipeline.

*To realize that God is all
and all is God gives
man courage. He does not
shrink.*

*The Lord does not favour
those who are not sincere and
honest.*

Chapter One
Hinduism: An Overview

The religion that has come to be known as Hinduism is certainly the oldest and most varied of all the great religions of the world. The word 'Hinduism' itself is a geographical term based upon the Sanskrit name for the great river, known as the Sindhu, that runs across the northern boundaries of India. For those living on the other side of this river, the entire region to the south-east of the Sindhu, which the Greeks called the Indus, came to be known as the land of the Hindus, and the vast spectrum of faiths that flourished here acquired the generic name Hinduism. In fact, Hinduism calls itself the *Sanatana Dharma,* the eternal faith, because it is based not upon the teachings of a single preceptor but on the collective wisdom and inspiration of great seers and sages from the very dawn of Indian civilisation.

The Scriptures

The Sanskrit word for philosophy is *darshana* or 'seeing', which implies that Hinduism is not based merely on intellectual speculation but is grounded upon direct and immediate perception. This, in fact, distinguishes Indian philosophy from much of Western philosophical thought. The oldest and most important scriptures of Hinduism are the *Vedas*, which contain inspired utterances of seers and sages who had achieved a direct perception of the divine being. The *Vedas* are considered to be eternal, because they are not merely superb poetic compositions but represent the divine truth itself as perceived through the elevated consciousness of great seers.

The four *Vedas*—the *Rig*, the *Yajur*, the *Sama* and the *Atharva*—contain between them over a hundred thousand verses, which include some of the greatest mystical poetry ever written. For example, the famous Hymn of Creation in the *Rig Veda* (X. 129/1 – 7) is an extraordinary utterance. It has been translated by Griffith as follows:

> Then was not non-existent nor existent:
> there was no realm of air, no sky beyond it:
> What covered it, and where? and what give shelter?
> Was water there, unfathomed depth of water?

Death was not then, nor was there aught immortal:
No sign was there, the day's and night's divider.
That One thing, breathless, breathed by its own nature:
apart from it was nothing whatsoever.

Darkness there was: at first concealed in darkness
this All was indiscriminate chaos.
All that existed then was void and formless:
by the great power of Warmth was born that Unit.

Thereafter rose Desire in the beginning,
Desire the primal seed and germ of Spirit.
Sages who searched with their hearts' thought discovered
the existent's kinship with the non-existent.

Transversely was their severing line extended:
what was above it then, and what below it?
There were begetters, there were mighty forces,
free action here and energy up yonder.

Who verily knows and who can here declare it,
whence it was born and whence comes this creation?
The gods are later than the world's production,
who knows then whence it first came into being?

He, the first origin of this creation,
whether he formed it all or did not form it,
Whose eye controls this world in highest heaven,
He verily knows it, or perhaps he knows not.

The *Vedas* contain beautiful hymns addressed to various powers of nature such as the Sun, the Moon, the Ocean, the Rain, the Dawn, all pervaded by a deep intuitive awareness of the essential unity and interconnectedness behind these phenomena. Portions deal with the ritual worship of the early Aryans, the *yajna* sacrifice revolving around the sacred fire which was looked upon as the intermediary between the human and the divine powers. There is also a fascinating array of medical prescriptions, specially in the *Atharva Veda,* and a great deal of other social material including hymns to matrimony and friendship, prayers for progeny, longevity, cattle and prosperity. Taken together, they constitute a unique document of the religious consciousness of all humanity. It is virtually a miracle that they came down intact through thousands of years entirely by memory, a fantastic feat of mnemonics for which countless generations of Brahmanas deserve unqualified gratitude. It was only in the middle of the nineteenth century that the great orientalist, Friedrich Max Müller, brought out the first printed edition of the *Rig Veda.*

The *Upanishads* are known as the *Vedanta*, or the end of the *Vedas* both, because they come at the end of the *Vedic* collections and also because they represent the culmination of *Vedic* teachings. One hundred and eight *Upanishads* have been preserved, of which at least 14 are of major importance. These remarkable dialogues between the teacher and one or more pupils deal with the deepest problems of human existence, of death and other realms of being, of the goal of life and the stages of spiritual realisation. The *Isha Upanishad,* though containing only 18 verses, is considered to be probably the most important such text. Its famous first line, 'This entire cosmos, whatever is still or moving, is pervaded by the divine', contains the very essence of Hinduism.

The *Mundaka Upanishad* (2.2.3) has a beautiful verse which brings out the essential role of the *Upanishads* as vehicles for spiritual realisations:

> Having taken as a bow the great weapon of the *Upanishads,* one should fix on it the arrow sharpened by constant meditation; drawing it with a mind filled with *That* (Brahman), penetrate, O handsome youth, the Imperishable as the target.

The *Katha Upanishad* contains the memorable dialogue between the boy Nachiketa and Yama, the God of Death, and represents a remarkable formulation of the *Vedantic* gospel. It is significant that in Hinduism death is not something to be looked upon with horror and hatred, but is rather considered to be as essential an aspect of existence as life, part of the inescapable dualities of day and night, heat and cold, good and evil, joy and sorrow that are woven into the very texture of manifested existence. It is only by transcending these dualities and attaining the *brahmasthiti*, the state of Brahman, that the human being can finally fulfil his cosmic destiny.

Contrary to a popular misconception often encountered in the West, Hinduism is not a passive, world-negating religion. It is verily a vibrant, life-affirming faith, using 'life' in the deeper sense of that supreme poise that transcends the dualities of life and death. According to the Hindu view, there is a supreme state into which it is possible for the human consciousness to enter and which, once achieved, places one above the endless cycle of rebirth in which the entire cosmos is imprisoned. The sage, Shvetashvatara, says in the great *Upanishad* that bears his name (3.8): 'I know that Great Being, effulgent like the Sun shining on the other shore beyond the darkness.' And Lord Krishna also describes the supreme goals as 'the light of all lights beyond the darkness' in the *Bhagavad Gita* (13. 17).

The attainment of this exalted state of consciousness is not incompatible with action in this world. While it is true that there has always been a significant stand of renunciation in Hinduism, which found fuller expression in the Jain and Buddhist traditions that flowed from the mother faith, it is useful to remember that the goal of Hinduism is a luminous, glowing state of supreme bliss, not a negative self-annihilation.

There are five basic tenets that underlie Hinduism which, if properly understood, provide the key to an understanding of a faith that is bewildering in its apparent diversity and complexity. The first is the concept of Brahman, the unchanging, undying reality that pervades the entire cosmos. The *Vedic* seers saw that everything in the universe changes, and they called the creation *samsara,* that which always moves. But they also perceived that behind this change there was an unchanging substratum from which the changing worlds emanated like sparks from a great fire. This supreme, all-pervasive entity known as Brahman has been beautifully described in various *Upanishads*. Thus the *Mundaka Upanishad* (2.2.12) has the following verse:

> Brahman verily is this immortal being.
> In front is Brahman, behind is Brahman.
> To the right and to the left.
> It spreads forth above and below.
> Verily, Brahman is this effulgent universe.

Similarly, the following important passage in the *Shvetashvatara Upanishad* (4.2-4) shows clearly that, although the Hindus worshipped many manifestations of the divine, they realised that behind them all there was the same all-pervasive Brahman:

> Thou art the fire.
> Thou art the sun,
> Thou art the air,
> Thou art the moon,
> Thou art the starry firmament,
> Thou art Brahman Supreme:
> Thou art the waters—Thou
> The creator of all!
>
> Thou art woman, thou art man,
> Thou art the youth, thou art the maiden,
> Thou art the old man tottering with his staff:
> Thou facest everywhere.
>
> Thou art the dark butterfly,
> Thou art the green parrot with red eyes,
> Thou art the thunder cloud, the seasons, the seas.
> Without beginning art thou.
> Beyond time, beyond space,
> Thou art he from whom sprang
> The three worlds.
>
> Filled with Brahman are the things we see;
> Filled with Brahman floweth all that is;
> From Brahman all—yet is he still the same.

The second great insight of the *Vedic* seers was that, as the changing universe outside was pervaded by the Brahman, the changing world within man himself was based upon the undying Atman. They realised that 'like corn, a mortal ripens and like corn is born again' (*Katha Upanishad*, 1.1.6). 'The human entity is born again and again across the aeons, gathering a multitude of experiences and gradually moving towards the possibility of perfection. This immortal spark they called the Atman'.

Having perceived the existence of the undying Brahman without and the undying Atman within, the great seers were able to make the critical leap of realising through their spiritual insight that the Atman and Brahman were essentially one. In the *Chhandogya Upanishad*, there is the famous story of Shvetaketu, who is taught by his father in a series of statements which end with the famous words *Tat tvam asi*—'That thou art'—meaning that the Atman was essentially the Brahman. What the exact relationship between the two is has been the basis of various great schools of *Vedanta*, some holding with Shankaracharya that in fact the two are identical (the *Advaita Vedanta*), some with Ramanujacharya that they are both unitary and dual (the *Vishishtadvaita*) and some with Madhavacharya that they are similar but always separate (the *Dvaita*).

Having established the existence of the Brahman, the Atman and their relationship, the fourth major tenet of Hinduism is that the supreme goal of life lies in spiritual realisation whereby the individual becomes aware of the deathless Atman within him. The realisation of the Atman at once brings an entirely new dimension into the picture, and the realised soul transcends the cycle of suffering, illness, old age and death which are inevitable concomitants of ordinary life, the wheel of change and decay of the manifested universe. He may still choose to stay within the limits of manifestations, and by his presence sweeten the bitter sea of suffering, but he is no longer bound to do so.

The fifth concept which lies at the very heart of the Hindu way of life is that of *karma*, a concept that includes action, causality and destiny. Action being inevitable, the human individual is bound by the results of his actions, pleasant fruits flowing from good deeds and unpleasant consequences from evil ones. *Karma* can thus be considered the moral equivalent of the law of conservation of energy or the equivalence of action and reaction in the field of natural sciences. While it is true that what we are today is the result of our past deeds, it also follows that we are the makers of our future by the way we act at present. Thus, far from implying fatalism as is often wrongly believed, *karma* gives tremendous responsibility to the individual and places in his own hands the key to his future destiny. Naturally, the unerring law of *karma* can work itself out only over a sufficiently long period of time; therefore the Hindu belief in reincarnation, with the Atman being reborn in a long series until the attainment of liberation. Indeed, if man were to have only one life, there would seem to be no moral or spiritual justification at all for the tremendous disparities and evidently undeserved suffering, even of children, which is so evident all around us. As the *Bhagavad Gita* (2.23) has it: 'As a man casts off his worn-out garments and takes others that are new, so that Atman casts off worn-out bodies and enters others that are new.'

The good man makes no distinction between friend and foe, brother and stranger, but regards them all with impartiality. A true friend will be sympathetic to you at all times.

Chapter Two

The Key Concepts

In addition to the *Vedas* and the *Upanishads*, Hinduism has a vast corpus of auxiliary scriptures including the two great epics, the *Ramayana* and the *Mahabharata*. Between them they express the collective wisdom and history of the entire race, and have had a profound influence on all aspects of Hindu life and culture in India and throughout Southeast Asia for thousands of years. Then there are eighteen *Puranas*, rich in myth and symbol, of which the best known is the *Shimad-Bhagavatam;* the *Brahma-Sutras* which contain *Vedantic* philosophy in the form of aphorisms, and the *Tantras* dealing with the esoteric aspects of the spiritual quest. There are also the codes of conduct, including the elaborate *Manu-Smriti,* which seeks to relate religion to the social and individual lives of Hindus.

Embedded within the huge compass of the *Mahabharata* is that crest jewel of Hindu thought and one of the great religious classics of mankind, the *Bhagavad Gita*. Before going into the teaching of the *Gita*, however, it will be useful to mention five sets of concepts which are an integral part of the Hindu ethos, as some understanding of these is essential if one is to grasp the main thrust of the teaching of the *Gita*. Briefly, the concepts are as follows.

The Four *Yugas* or Cycles of Time

The Hindu concept of time is cyclical, not linear. The universe is *anadi-ananta*, without beginning and without end, going through recurrent phases of manifestation and dissolution. It is quite extraordinary how the Hindu concept of time is becoming more comprehensible with recent developments in extragalactic cosmology. Each day of Brahma, the creator principle in the Hindu trinity, consists of four billion, three hundred and twenty million years, and the night of Brahma is of a similar duration. Thus, the entire universe is a process of the outbreathing and inbreathing of Brahma, corresponding to alternating periods of manifestation and dissolution. Each manifested cycle is divided into four *yugas* or aeons—*Satya, Treta, Dvapara* and *Kali*. In the

Satya-yuga, virtue is in the ascendant, but this diminishes progressively until in the *Kali-yuga* it virtually disappears. At the end of each *Kali-yuga,* there is tremendous destruction, *pralaya,* after which the golden age appears again. The four *yugas* taken together form a *Maha-yuga* or a great cycle. We are now believed to be living in the *Kali-yuga* of the present cycle.

The Four *Ashramas* or Stages of Life

In the Hindu view human life is divided into four *ashramas* or stages—*Brahmacharya, Grihastha, Vanaprastha* and *Sannyasa.* As the ideal lifespan of the Hindus was a hundred years, each of these stages consists of twenty-five-year period. The first twenty-five years would be student life, when the young man is expected to spend his time and energy upon the attainment of education at the feet of a qualified teacher, and to observe sexual abstinence. Once this is completed, he moves on to the *Grihastha ashrama,* or householder stage, wherein he marries, raises a family and participates in economically productive activity for the welfare of society. By fifty, he is ready to move on to the *Vanaprastha* stage of semi-retirement, in which he gradually brings himself to detach himself from worldly activities and to concentrate upon the study of scriptures and meditational practices. Finally, at seventy-five, he is ready to withdraw entirely from social life and becomes a *sannyasi* or ascetic by renouncing the world, freeing himself from all social responsibilities and concentrating exclusively upon the spiritual quest. *Sannyasa ashrama,* however, can be entered into even at a younger age by a person who renounces worldly life and joins one of the many monastic orders that exist in Hinduism.

The Four *Purusharthas* or Goals of Life

According to Hindu thought, these four goals are *dharma, artha, kama* and *moksha. Dharma* is a word that has often been translated as 'religion', but, in fact, it is more comprehensive. It implies not only a religious and philosophical framework but a total worldview, including a scheme of right conduct under various circumstances. It comes from the root *dhri,* which means to uphold, and in the broadest sense is used for the universal laws of nature that uphold the cosmos. It also implies such concepts as justice, virtue, morality, righteousness, law and duty. It is the first of the four goals, because it is the most comprehensive and is valid throughout the life of a human being.

Artha, or wealth, is the second goal. It is interesting that Hinduism not only tolerates the importance of wealth but accepts it positively as one of the four main goals of life, provided its acquisition and utilisation are in accord with the enjoyment. Here again, Hinduism gives an important place to sensual enjoyment, realising that, while renunciation may be suitable for the ascetic, it is certainly not suited to the common man. Therefore, the concept of *kama* is incorporated in the Hindu ethos, and indeed it has its own shastra in the form of the famous *Kama-Sutra* by Vatsyayana. The final goal in Hindu thought is *moksha,* or release from suffering, old age and ultimately from death itself. As mentioned earlier, *moksha* is not simply a question of survival after death, which in any case is taken for granted in Hinduism: it implies transcending both life and death by the attainment of that spiritual poise whereby man is liberated from the wheel of *samsara.*

The Four *Varnas* or Castes

According to the traditional Hindu view, human beings are divided into four categories on the basis of their intrinsic qualities. The highest caste consists of Brahmin, the thinkers, philosophers, priests, whose role it is to provide spiritual guidance and intellectual sustenance to society. Next come the Kshatriyas, or warriors, whose *dharma* revolves around ruling the nation and defending it against aggression. Third are the Vaishyas, or traders, who are involved in agricultural and commercial operations, while all that falls within the sphere of service is the responsibility of the fourth category of Shudras, or labourers. It is interesting that the word *varna* also means colour, and, if one looks back over the history of early India, it is clear that the problem of colour as between the Aryans, the great existing Dravidian civilisation, and the numerous aboriginal tribes was a major factor in the development of this caste concept. There were certain categories beyond the pale of the caste system which were known as the outcastes, and whose ill-treatment over the centuries is a standing disgrace to the otherwise remarkable achievements of Hindu civilisation.

The Four *Yogas* or Paths to the Divine

The word *yoga* is derived from the root *yuj,* meaning to join or yoke, and it involves the joining of the Atman with the Brahman, of the individual soul with the universal divine being. In the Hindu view, there are several methods of this union, and each spiritual aspirant chooses the one that is best suited to his inner and outer conditions. While the path is essentially one, it varies to the extent that emphasis is placed upon different human faculties. Over the ages, four main *yogas* or paths have developed—*jnana, bhakti, karma* and *raja. Jnana* is the path of intellectual discrimination, suitable for those whose intellects are highly developed and who are taught constantly to discriminate between the real and the unreal, the ephemeral and the eternal, until they reach spiritual realisation. *Bhakti,* or the path of devotion to a personal form of God, is based on the emotional urge, and involves harnessing of the sovereign power of love to spiritual quest. In this path, there is a deep emotional relationship between the human and the divine, beautifully expressed by Arjuna in the *Gita* as the combined relationship of a father to a son, a friend to a dear friend and a lover to his beloved. *Karma,* or the way of action, is best suited for people who are particularly drawn by social service, alleviation of human suffering and organisational activity, and whose constant compulsion for work is directed towards the divine. Finally, *Raja-yoga* involves various spiritual practices, including physical and psychic exercises set out in Patanjali's classic, the *Yoga-Sutra*. These paths are by no means mutually exclusive, and can, indeed, enjoy a benign symbiosis.

Another important aspect of Hindu thought is the concept of the *avatara,* or descent of God in human form. In keeping with its concept of cyclic time, Hinduism holds that there have been numerous such descents in the past and will be more in the future. As Krishna himself says in the *Gita* (4.7—8):

> Whensoever righteousness declines, O Bharata, and unrighteousness arises, then do I manifest myself upon earth. For the deliverance of the good, for the destruction of evil-doers and for the re-establishment of righteousness, I am born from age to age.

With these concepts in mind, we can now turn to the *Bhagavad Gita*. The teaching of the *Upanishads* is in a peaceful setting, usually in the forest *ashramas* or retreats of the teacher. The setting of the *Bhagavad Gita,* however, is entirely different. Here the teacher and the disciple—Shri Krishna and Arjuna— are placed in the very centre of the battlefield. The conches have been sounded, the flight of missiles has begun and, poised between the two armies, Arjuna suddenly suffers a failure of nerves when he sees arrayed against him, his kinsmen and teachers. He is overcome by a great wave of revulsion, and at that critical juncture implores his friend and teacher to show him the correct path. The setting of the *Gita* is thus similar to the present human predicament. Man today finds himself in the midst of serious conflicts, both outer and inner; and it is on the battlefield of life that he needs correct guidance. This explains the special appeal of the *Gita* to modern man.

Another unique feature of the *Gita* is that it fuses the four paths into a single integral movement towards the divine. It deals with all the four *yogas,* but constantly seeks to integrate them around the overriding relationship between Arjuna and Shri Krishna, the human and the divine. While the Brahman of the *Upanishads* is impersonal and is, therefore, referred to as 'That', in the *Gita,* Shri Krishna himself appears as the Divine Being that transcends both the manifest and the unmanifest in his all-encompassing consciousness. The divine in the *Gita* is not a non-personalised concept, but involves the personality, raised as it were to the nth degree. Thus at the end of the teaching, Shri Krishna instructs Arjuna in these words (18.61 – 2):

> The Lord, O Arjuna, is seated in the heart of all beings,
> causing by His divine power the entire cosmos
> to revolve as if mounted on a machine.
> Take refuge in Him with your entire being, O Bharata;
> by His Grace you will gain supreme peace and the
> eternal abode.

Having thus spoken of the divine in the third person, Krishna completes the teaching with the following memorable verse (18.65 – 6):

> Fix your mind on Me, be devoted to Me,
> Sacrifice to Me, bow to Me and to Me shall you come.

This is My pledge to you, for you are dear to Me.
Abandon all dharmas and take refuge in Me alone.
Fear not, I will deliver you from all sin.

The *Bhagavad Gita* is a remarkable fount of inspiration and power. Among its many memorable passages is the famous scene in the Eleventh Chapter where Krishna reveals to Arjuna his Divine Form which encompasses the entire cosmos and yet includes the great calm that lies behind all manifestation. It is this vision that is described as having the splendour of a thousand suns risen simultaneously in the sky. The *Gita* also contains the celebrated and oft-quoted statement with regard to action and its fruit. While man should work constantly for the welfare of the world, he should not be attached to the fruits of his action and should repose them in the divine. The *Gita* thus teaches unceasing involvement in action while retaining an inner core of detachment, and dedicating the totality of human life to the divine will. Involvement without obsession is the key concept.

While there are many *avataras* in the Hindu scriptures, including manifestations of Shiva in the South Indian tradition, the best known list is a set of ten incarnations of Vishnu known as the *Dashavatara*. They have had a profound influence on popular Hinduism, and include two of the most popular and widely worshipped figures in the Hindu pantheon, Rama and

Krishna. Interestingly, these ten incarnations represent the evolutionary ladder in a most remarkable manner. They start with Matsya the fish; then Kurma, the amphibious tortoise; then Varaha, the boar; then Narasimha, the man-lion; then Vamana, the dwarf; then Parashurama, the wielder of the great axe; then Shri Rama, the noble hero of the *Ramayana;* then Shri Krishna, the divine flutist; and incarnation of this cycle yet to manifest, the Kalki *avatara,* depicted as a magnificent youth riding a great white horse with a meteor-like sword raining death and destruction on all sides, perhaps symbolising some cataclysmic nuclear conflict.

The inclusion of the Buddha as the ninth incarnation needs special comment, because it reveals the great capacity in Hinduism to absorb even heretical movements. Evidently the fame and influence of the Buddha were so great that he could not be ignored, and yet his teachings were in some respects antithetical to classical Hinduism. He was, therefore, absorbed into the Hindu pantheon, so that he is revered today by Hindus with no difficulty at all. Indeed, although technically the number of Buddhists in India is very small, this is partly due to the fact that many of his teachings, such as his stern condemnation of animal sacrifice, have become part of the Hindu mainstream itself. To some extent, the same can be said about Christ, and most Hindus have no difficulty in accepting him as one of the incarnations of God. What Hinduism is not able to accept is the exclusive claim of any one teacher to the monopoly of divinity and wisdom for all time to come.

Chapter Three
Classical Hinduism

With the *Vedas*, the *Upanishads* and the auxiliary scriptures culminating in the *Bhagavad Gita,* the major contours of Hinduism became clearly defined. But in Hinduism there has been through the last two thousand years a continuous process of reinterpretation and restatement by a series of remarkable men and women. Some were kings and erudite scholars, others were common folk, often unlettered and unsophisticated. Some belonged to the 'higher' Brahmin, Kshatriya and Vaishya castes, others to the 'lower', including the 'outcastes'. Some spoke chaste Sanskrit, that most magnificent of human languages; others sang in the local dialects. Some lived in great palaces and temples; others in simple cottages, or roamed the countryside with neither home nor shelter. Some were devoted to Shiva, the great Lord seated in majestic solitude on the mountain peak; some to Krishna, the eternal lover playing his divine flute in the forests of Vrindavana. Some worshipped the great Mother in one of her innumerable forms, beauty enthroned upon the seat of power; others offered their homage to one or the other numerous deities in the Hindu pantheon, rich with an inexhaustible store of symbol and image.

And yet, running through all these remarkable persons like a golden thread, is the overriding common factor—their realisation of the divine. Hinduism has always reserved its deepest veneration for those who have in some way realised the divine. Scholars are respected, rulers are feared, but real veneration is reserved only for the realised ones who constitute a race apart, the race that never dies. And it is a remarkable fact, largely responsible for the continued vitality of Hinduism through the ages, that it has in every century produced a number of such realised souls. Spread from Kashmir in the North to Kerala in the South, from Gujarat in the West to Assam in the East, these great souls have by the sheer force of their spiritual realisation kept the inner power of Hinduism intact and reillumined Hindu society in times of incredible adversity and ordeal. Had it not been for these great ones, truly the salt of the earth, Hinduism which had to undergo such savage persecution for centuries would have vanished from the face of this earth.

The Great Acharyas

Space permits only a rapid survey of the more important developments in Hinduism over the last twenty centuries. The first outstanding figure that comes to mind is Tiruvalluvar (c. AD 300), the great Tamil saint, whose classic work, the *Tirukkural,* is generally known as the *Veda* of the Tamils. Then came Adi Shankaracharya (*b.* AD 686), the extraordinary philosopher from Kerala, who wrote illuminating commentaries on the great Hindu texts, innumerable hymns to various deities in beautiful Sanskrit, and a number of treatises on the philosophy of non-dualism or *Advaita Vedanta*. He also founded four *pithas* or monastic centres in the four corners of India—at Shringeri in the South, Dwarika in the West, Badrinatha in the North and Puri in the East—which have played a profound role in sustaining classical Hinduism down the ages. Shankara stressed the supreme importance of liberation achieved through knowledge which, in turn, is born of asceticism and meditation. In his system, devotion and action could only play a preparatory and subsidiary role.

In sharp contradistinction to Shankara's monistic philosophy was the theistic approach of the great Tamil scholar Ramanuja (*b*. AD 1017) who advocated qualified monism and proclaimed that the way of devotion was the supreme path. The seeker must develop a devotion to God so intense that he realises that he is only a fragment of Him and wholly dependent on His grace. Thus Ramanuja held that, however high the individual soul may rise, it will always remain in some degree separate from the divine, so that the intense interpersonal relationship can subsist for ever.

Another great South Indian Acharya was Madhava (*b*. AD 1199), whose system can be described as dualistic in that he held that God and individual souls are eternally distinct, and the salvation consists not in the merger of the two but in the soul dwelling eternally close to God and enjoying the contemplation of His glory. Madhava also held a doctrine, not generally found in Hinduism, that souls who consistently indulge in evil can ultimately get so weighed down that they can be permanently expelled from the universe to a state of eternal damnation.

These great teachers and their followers wrote original commentaries upon the *prasthanatrayi,* the three foundations of Hindu philosophy—the *Upanishads*, the *Brahma-Sutras* and the *Bhagavad Gita*. In addition, for intellectual and academic classification, Hindu philosophy has been divided into six systems of thought, each associated with a great teacher, which are generally reduced to three categories. The *Vaisheshika* of Kanada and the *Nyaya* of Gautama form one group; the *Sankhya* of Kapila and the *Yoga* of Patanjali the second; and the *Purva-Mimamsa* of Jaimini and the *Vedanta* (also called *Uttara-Mimamsa*) of Vyasa the third. These schools are regarded as *astika* or orthodox, because they accept the overriding authority of the *Vedas*, while the two other great schools of Indian philosophy, Jainism (whose twenty-fourth great teacher, Mahavira, lived in the sixth century BC) and Buddhism (founded by Gautama Buddha in the same century) are regarded as *anastika* or heterodox because they repudiate the authority of the *Vedas*.

Almost contemporaneous with these great sons of Indian spiritual movements there developed in the northernmost state of Kashmir a unique and extremely rich tradition, known to the world as Kashmir Shaivism. Based on the *Tantras*—esoteric spiritual texts—rather than the *Vedas*, it produced a series of great teachers, the most outstanding of whom was Acharya Abhinavagupta (BC AD 950—975) who must rank as one of the greatest spiritual masters in the entire Hindu tradition.

Chapter Four

The Forms of the Formless

It is necessary to point out, however, that while learned scholars proclaimed and disputed these various schools of philosophy, for the common man, the mainstay of Hinduism has always been devotion to a deity representing some aspect or incarnation of the divine. Hinduism has a wealth of imagery, symbolism and iconography, and has produced a dazzling array of images and concepts which often baffles non-Hindus. This has led to the erroneous view, still extant in some quarters, that Hinduism is polytheistic. It certainly encourages the worship of many forms and symbols, but it must be understood that behind these myriad forms is the same all-pervasive divinity mirrored in a thousand different ways.

Very briefly, popular Hindu worship today revolves around three major deities—Shiva, Vishnu as himself and his major incarnations, and the goddess. Shiva Mahadeva is the great primeval lord, and there is reason to believe that he is of a pre-Aryan origin because on the still undeciphered seals of the Indus Valley Civilisation (*c.* 5000—3000 BC), there is a figure seated cross-legged with several of the features associated with Shiva. Shiva is invariably worshipped along with a *lingam,* a powerful symbol representing the creative force behind all manifestation. He is generally portrayed as a resplendent ascetic sitting in meditation on a mountain peak, his body smeared with ashes, deadly snakes entwined around his neck, and the sacred Ganges flowing from his matted locks. He is also worshipped in his role as the cosmic dancer, Nataraja, whose dance symbolises the eternal wheel of the cosmos where millions of worlds are destroyed every moment and millions other spring into existence to the best of the eternal rhythm. Indeed, the magnificent image of the dancing Shiva represents one of the high watermarks of human art.

Despite his fearsome appearance, Shiva (the very word means 'auspicious') is easy to please, Ashutosha, and is generous with his boons even to the titans who often misuse them. He is neither born nor does he die, being the master of birth and death. In south India, there is a tradition in which Shiva is believed to have appeared in human form on several different occasions, either to help his devotees or to impart esoteric teachings. He is the *maha-yogi,* the great ascetic, and the patron-saint of those practising *yoga.*

Shiva is the third god of the Hindu trinity—Brahma the creator, Vishnu the preserver and Shiva the destroyer—but again it must be remembered that these are not three different gods but three aspects of the same divine being. This is beautifully portrayed in the magnificent monolithic sculpture of *Trimurti* on the Elephant Island off the coast of Mumbai. One of the world's great artistic creations, this massive sculpture shows clearly the three aspects integrated in a single, divine entity. In fact, the great art of India provides as useful a way of approaching an understanding of the theistic concepts as the texts themselves. Apart from sculpture and painting, the great classical dance forms of India, particularly the Bharatanatyam, can bring to life concepts which may appear abstruse and unidimensional when approached purely through the written word.

Vishnu is depicted as lying on a great serpent that floats on the vast, endless ocean of milk, the *kshirasagara.* In this form he is worshipped in many temples, specially in the South, but elsewhere in India he is more widely worshipped in two of his most popular incarnations associated with the two great epics—Shri Rama and Shri Krishna. Indeed, these two names have carried the undying message of Hinduism to billions of men and women for thousands of years now, not only in India but wherever the Hindu cultural impact has been felt in the world. Shri Rama is depicted with a bow in hand, accompanied by his noble wife Sita, his faithful brother Lakshmana, and his devoted follower, the monkey god, Hanuman. Shri Krishna is depicted in numerous forms, commencing with his early childhood as a baby, Bala Krishna, and terminating as the charioteer of Arjuna, Parthasarathi. But his most popular and appealing form is as a beautiful cowherd youth, Gopala Krishna, dark and resplendent, standing with one foot crossed over the other and playing his magic flute. He is generally worshipped along with Radha, the shepherdess who has come to symbolise the essence of the Krishna cult of devotion. Vishnu is also worshipped in some of his lesser known incarnations such as Narasimha, the man-lion, who appeared to rid the world of the demon-king, Hiranyakashipu, and save his son, the great boy-devotee Prahlada.

The third major focus of devotion in India is the goddess in her numerous forms. She is worshipped as Parvati, the consort of Shiva; Lakshmi, the consort of Vishnu; Sita and Radha along with Shri Rama and Shri Krishna. But, and this is a point of considerable significance, she is not only worshipped as a consort, but in her own right as the essence of power and beauty; as Durga with eighteen arms riding a lion and scattering the demon hordes like chaff; as Kali, the fierce, naked goddess standing upon a corpse and drinking the blood of her freshly slain enemies; as Saraswati, the goddess of art, poetry and music, the patron of all learning and wisdom. The worship of the great mother is, of course, known throughout the world in one form or another, but it is in Hinduism that she appears in all her splendour.

There is a Pauranic myth about the birth of Durga which is full of symbolic significance. Once a great demon, the buffalo-headed Mahishasura, representing the evil forces of brute materialism, succeeded in defeating all the gods (*devas*: the shining ones) and established his supremacy over creation. The gods despaired, because despite all their efforts, they could not vanquish this terrible monster. At last they gathered together on a mountain peak and decided to pool their divine powers. Each god contributed his own power symbolised by a weapon, led by the lord of the gods, Indra. At the end of the great ritual, when all the divine powers had been pooled, there arose a dazzling light which spread its glory throughout the three worlds. In the midst of the light appeared Durga, the great goddess, with a weapon in each of her eighteen arms, and riding a ferocious tiger. She then gave battle to Mahishasura, and after a terrible conflict lasting nine days and nine nights, she finally slew him and rid the world of this great terror. These nine nights, the Navaratri, are still celebrated every year by Hindus as symbolising the victory of divine power over the forces of evil.

In addition to Shiva, Vishnu and the goddess, there are numerous other deities who are the object of devotion and worship by Hindus down to the present day. These include the elephant-headed Ganesha, remover of obstacles, whose worship is essential before any auspicious undertaking can begin; Kartikeya or Subrahmanya, the younger son of Shiva and Parvati who is widely worshipped in South India as a young boy with a spear, riding a peacock; Hanuman, the devoted follower of Shri Rama who, despite his simian appearance, is wise and powerful; Dattatreya, the three-headed deity who is the patron-saint of *yogis* engaged in esoteric practices; and Ayappan, a South Indian deity, believed to be the result of a union between Shiva and Vishnu in his female form as Mohini. Surya, the sun-god, is known as the *pratyaksha-deva,* the visible god, and is generally worshipped through the famous *gayatri mantra.* Curiously, Brahma, the first god of the Hindu trinity, has only one temple in Pushkar dedicated to him in the whole of India, his worship having evidently fallen into disuse along with that of the other *Vedic* gods such as Indra and Varuna.

An important point to remember is that the worship of these various deities is by no means mutually exclusive. While each Hindu usually has a special family deity—the *ishta-devata*— he often worships three or four different deities during his daily prayers, and pays homage to any deity in a temple he may visit. Also, apart from anthropomorphic deities, some Hindus in addition use certain symbols for purposes of meditation. The most important of these is the *Aum* which is described in the scriptures as being the audio-visual symbol of Brahman itself, and is endowed with a wealth of symbolism. An entire *Upanishad—Mandukya—*has been devoted to the word *Aum.*

Meditation on the symbol and sound of *Aum* is an important aspect of *yoga,* a word that has gained much currency of late throughout the world but is generally imperfectly understood. As has been mentioned earlier, *yoga* implies the joining or yoking of human consciousness to the Divine Being, and in this sense it can be applied to the four major paths of spiritual attainment. In a more specialised sense, *yoga* involves physical and mental disciplines directed at control over mental and physical functions, specially breathing. The classic text of this *yoga* is the celebrated *Yoga-Sutra* of Patanjali, one of the world's great religious classics.

The *sutras,* or aphorisms of Patanjali, lay down an eight fold path, *ashtanga-yoga* of physical, psychological and moral discipline that, if properly adhered to under the guidance of a qualified teacher, results in the consciousness of the seeker being gradually elevated until the Atman shines forth in its pristine glory as pure consciousness. This path also involves arousal of the *kundalini shakti* or serpent power, believed to be located at the base of the human spine. As this power rises through a series of occult centres or *chakras* located in various parts of the body, the consciousness is correspondingly elevated, until finally it bursts into the highest *chakra* at the top of the brain—the *sahasrara* or thousand-petalled lotus—where the merger between the Atman and the Brahman takes place and the seeker is plunged into the highest bliss. This elevated state, known as *samadhi,* is the goal of all *yogic* practices.

Numerous other texts on various aspects of *yoga* are to be found in Hindu literature, all basing themselves upon the foundations laid by Patanjali. These include the *Tantras* or esoteric texts which deal with the various practices and techniques of *kundalini* arousal and acquisition of psychic powers. These miraculous powers, or *siddhis,* are accepted as an important aspect of *yogic* practices, but their misuse or even excessive demonstration is frowned upon as a hindrance to the achievement of the supreme goal. Through the ages, as today, there have been in India a fair number of persons who possess these powers, and miracle-mongering has always been an occupational hazard for *yogis* which it is not always easy to avoid.

An important aspect of Hinduism, whether it is *yoga* or any other system of philosophy, discipline or teaching, is the critical importance that is assigned to the *guru* or teacher. The *guru* in the Hindu tradition is to be venerated even more than one's parents, because while our parents give us physical life, it is the *guru* who brings about our spiritual rebirth whereby alone can man fulfil his cosmic destiny. This notion, which appears to many to be somewhat exaggerated, will become clearer when it is understood that the human *guru* is but a symbol of the divine power that already resides within us. The word *guru* itself means dispeller of darkness, and by bringing the light of spiritual wisdom into the material darkness of normal human consciousness, the *guru* indeed performs a unique and priceless function.

Needless to say, in Hinduism, as in so many other religions, there is the usual quota of charlatans and even criminals masquerading under the guise and habit of spiritual teachers. Generally, a person gets the sort of *guru* he deserves, and there is a well-established tradition that when the disciple is ready, the *guru* will appear. In the *Mundaka Upanishad* two essential qualifications of a true *guru* are laid down, both of which must be fulfilled if a person is really to occupy that elevated status. The *guru* must be *shrotriya,* learned in the scriptures, and *brahmanishtha* established in the Brahman or divine consciousness. Hinduism believes that spiritual attainment is not possible without a *guru,* although sometimes in place of a human *guru,* a book or scripture may suffice. There have also been instances in which people have been initiated by some high being through a dream rather than in the flesh.

Chapter Five

The Bhakti Movement

Despite great turmoil for many centuries in the North, due to foreign invasions and conquests, Hinduism continued to develop. Indeed, an important aspect of its development during Muslim rule was a two fold movement: a turning inwards to preserve itself in the face of widespread, often severe, persecution by Muslims whose religion forbade many of the practices central to Hinduism, specially image-worship; and a syncretic movement in which at the mystical level there could be a synthesis between the two faiths. Both these factors led to a tremendous devotional revival which has collectively come to be known as the Bhakti movement, one of the most interesting movements in the long and eventful history of Hinduism.

Throughout the Middle Ages there arose a series of extraordinary saint-singers who preached the gospel of divine love and ecstasy. While previous Hindu teachings had been almost exclusively in Sanskrit, this new movement broke away from the rigid and conservative Brahmin-dominated tradition, and used the regional languages and dialects to propagate their message. This also involved a revolt against the rigid caste restrictions and taboos that had become a negative feature in classical Hinduism. The saint-singers not only came from all castes and communities, including Muslims and some remarkable women, but their message was addressed to the common people irrespective of caste or creed.

In Islam also, as against the *ulama* or clergy, there has always been a mystical tradition of seekers intoxicated with the love of God. These were known as Sufis, and it was with the Sufi tradition that the Bhakti movement developed close affinity. The first major Sufi teacher to come to India was the great Khwaja Moinuddin Chishti (*b.* 1142). He arrived in Delhi towards the end of the twelfth century, and finally settled in Ajmer where he had many disciples, both Hindu and Muslim. His great shrine there, the Dargah Shareef, is today one of the most important centres of Muslim pilgrimage, and draws numerous Hindu pilgrims also year after year. In Hinduism the first great figure of medieval mysticism was Ramananda (*c.*1370-1440). Although a disciple of Ramanuja, Ramananda moved away from traditional orthodoxy, challenged caste divisions and began preaching in Hindi rather than in Sanskrit. One of his most illustrious disciples was Guru Ravidas who was a cobbler by profession. By sheer dint of spiritual merit, he rose to become one of the most respected religious teachers of his time, and still has millions of followers.

Ramananda's disciples came mainly from the lower castes, the most famous being Kabir, who is claimed both by the Hindus and the Muslims. The son of a Muslim weaver, Kabir (1440-1518) was drawn into the Bhakti movement at an early age. His songs struck at the roots of religious orthodoxy, ritualism and intolerance. Kabir combined in himself the best of the Sufi and Bhakti traditions. One of his songs (translated by Rabindranath Tagore) contains the following stanzas:

O servant, where dost thou seek me?
O! I am beside thee.
I am neither in the temple nor in mosque;
I am neither in Kaaba nor in Kailasha,
Neither am I in rites and ceremonies,
Nor in yoga and renunciation.
If thou art a true seeker

Thou shalt at once see me,
Thou shalt meet me in a moment of time.
Kabir says, O Sadhu, God is the breath of all breath,
There is nothing but water at the holy bathing places,
I know that they are useless, for I have bathed in them,
The images are all lifeless, they cannot speak.
I know, for I have cried aloud to them.
The Purana and the Koran are mere words;
Lifting up the curtain, I have seen.
Kabir gives utterance to the words of experience;
He knows well that all other things are untrue.

Kabir had a tremendous influence upon the India of his day. Despite the fact that he was a lowly weaver, the sheer force of his spiritual realisation made him a focus of great veneration. There is an interesting, perhaps apocryphal, story about his death. Both the Hindus and the Muslims claimed his body, the former insisting that he be cremated and the latter that he be buried. When the shroud was removed, however, the body had disappeared and in its place was a heap of flowers. These were then divided between the contending parties; the Hindus carried off their share and cremated them with great devotion, while the Muslims buried their share with equal veneration. Thus, in death as in life Kabir taught the gospel of spiritual communion and brotherhood to India's two largest religious communities.

Kabir had many disciples, but two teachers who were greatly influenced by him deserve special mention. The first was Nanak (1469-1538) who went on to found the Sikh faith. He constantly emphasized that in the sight of God, 'there was no Hindu and no Mussalman', and many of the hymns contained in the *Granth Sahib,* the sacred book of the Sikhs, echo this concept. Another of Kabir's followers was Dadu (1544-1603) who also founded a powerful movement based on his teachings known as Dadupanth. He wrote many beautiful hymns, and in one of them he says:

God is my ancestor, the creator is my kinsman,
The world-guru is my caste, I am a child of the Almighty.

The Bhakti movement produced a profusion of great literature. Two figures of particular importance in the vast Hindi-speaking Indo-Gangetic plain are Tulsidasa (1527-1623) and Suradasa (1478-1581). Tulsidasa produced the first and greatest classic in Hindi, the *Ramacharitamanasa* (Holy Lake of Rama's Deeds), which is the story of the *Ramayana* retold in Hindi verse with a wealth of poetry and deep devotion. There are many versions of the *Ramayana,* the most important being the original Sanskrit version of Valmiki and the Tamil version of Kamban. But the *Ramacharitamanasa* has had a unique impact. For millions of Hindus in North India, it has provided for centuries the main cultural and religious foundations, and down to this day verses from it are sung in every village and town. It was this great religious classic that the indentured labourers, who went from India to Fiji, Surinam, Mauritius and other plantations during colonial rule, took with them, and which remains their religious umbilical cord linking them to the land of their origin. Tulsidasa looks upon Shri Rama as the supreme incarnation of the divine being, born for the salvation of mankind, and worthy of total devotion and dedication.

Suradasa, considered by some critics to be an even greater poet, became blind in early childhood. None the less, he composed beautiful devotional poetry directed towards Shri Krishna. The descriptions of Krishna's childhood, his youthful pranks, his dalliance with the *gopis* (milkmaids) of Vrindavana, his magical feats, his resplendent personality epitomising the Divine lover who summons human souls to the golden notes of his eternal flute, are part of the great heritage of Hinduism. Both Tulsidasa and Suradasa, along with a number of other devotional saints including the Pathan Raskhan, another devotee of Shri Krishna, gave a tremendous boost to popular Hinduism. At a time when Muslim rule was being established over most of India, and the older, classical orthodoxy was losing its hold upon the people's minds, the Bhakti movement once again demonstrated the resilience of Hinduism and its capacity to enable its followers to restate and reinterpret the eternal verities in the light of changed circumstances.

In Karnataka, the great saint Purandaradasa (1480-1564) sang of the glory of God and won a vast following. Eastern India, particularly Bengal, has always been an important centre of Hinduism. The great eleventh-century poet-devotee Jayadeva, who composed one of the post-classical Sanskrit masterpieces in his poem, the *Gita-Govinda,* relating the story of Shri Krishna, had given a great fillip to Vaishnava worship in Bengal and Orissa. An extraordinary saint called Chaitanya (1485-1534), popularly known as Mahaprabhu (the Great Lord), and considered by his devotees to be an incarnation of Shri Krishna himself, founded the Vaishnava movement in Bengal. A special feature of his ministry was the *kirtanas,* choral singing and chanting by groups of devotees wandering from village to village and from town to town. Often the men involved in chanting would be carried away by a religious frenzy, and Shri Chaitanya himself would be thrown into a trance or fit of ecstasy as he contemplated the glory of Krishna. Although he did not write extensively, he exerted a profound influence on the subsequent development of Bengali and Oriya literature. Further east in the Brahmaputra Valley, another great teacher and reformer,

Shankaradeva (1449-1568), writing in Assamese, greatly influenced the Hindus of that region. The same is true of Tukarama (1607-1649) in Maharashtra, which had earlier produced the young saint Jnaneshvara (1275-1296) whose Marathi work, the *Jnaneshvari,* is one of the great classics of Hinduism.

No survey of the Bhakti movement, howsoever brief, can omit the names of two remarkable women who have left the impress of their attainment upon future generations. Lalleshvari (1317-1372) was a Kashmiri saint who attained God-realisation at an early age, and whose life is full of legends and stories of miracles. Her utterances teach the direct path of realisation through intense love of the divine, renouncing attachment to worldly possessions and family ties, and rising above the dualities of caste and creed. She writes:

> Shiva abides in all that is everywhere;
> Then do not discriminate
> Between a Hindu and a Mussalman.
> If thou art wise, know thyself;
> That is the true knowledge of the Lord.
> I renounced fraud, untruth, deceit;
> I taught my mind to see the One
> In all my fellowmen.

How could I then discriminate
Between man and man
And not accept the food
Offered to me by brother man?

The other great woman figure of the Bhakti movement was Mirabai (1450-1512), a Rajput princess who was married at an early age to the Rana of Udaipur. She was a childhood devotee of Shri Krishna, and had dedicated her life to him. After her marriage, she continued to devote her entire time to the worship of Krishna, incurring the displeasure of her husband who even tried to poison her. By Krishna's grace, however, the cup of poison turned into honey as she danced in ecstasy before the image of the god. Mira subsequently renounced her worldly life, and wandered through India singing her beautiful compositions, which are among the most moving devotional songs of Hinduism. One of her best loved hymns goes thus:

Tying anklets upon her feet, Mira dances in ecstasy.
People say Mira has gone mad,
Her mother-in-law says she has disgraced the clan,
The Rana sent her a cup of poison
Which Mira, laughingly, drank.
I have myself become the eternal maid-servant of
My Narayana.
Mira's God is Giridhar, lifter of the mountain.

O Indestructible One, meet me swiftly in your
Eternal embrace.

Thus we see that in its most difficult period Hinduism produced a glittering galaxy of saint-singers drawn from all corners of the country, who inspired millions by their devotion and poetry, presented in an idiom readily understood by the masses. They were re-stating the great *Vedantic* truths—the unity of Atman and Brahman, of the human and the divine—in a new phraseology which took the message down to the most humble villages where the majority of Hindus have always lived. Their songs remain to this day a major source of inspiration for Hindus, and while the sonorous Sanskrit chanting of the magnificent *Vedic* hymns can still be heard on special occasions, specially in South India, it is the songs of the medieval saints which echo and re-echo in fields and forests, in villages and towns. Truly it has been said that music has the unique capacity to carry the human consciousness out of its narrow confines towards the brimming ocean of the divine.

Chapter Six
The Modern Renaissance

The entire history of Hinduism, looked at from a certain angle, can be seen as a constant process of challenge and response. To each major crisis, Hinduism reacted, first by briefly withdrawing into a shell, and then, with its unparalleled capacity for assimilation and regeneration, by a new resurgence. This happened with the Jain and Buddhist movements, with the early Christian missionaries and, to a lesser extent, with the Muslim advent. But with the arrival of the British, first as traders and finally as imperial rulers, Hinduism was confronted with the most critical of all the challenges it had faced in its long and eventful history.

By the time the British arrived in India, Hinduism had reached perhaps its lowest ebb. All sorts of superstitions and undesirable practices flourished in the name of religion. Caste taboos had become so rigid that Hindu society, which a thousand years earlier had sent its great missionaries to the four corners of Asia, had begun to insist on anyone returning from abroad having to undergo purificatory rites. Women, who once enjoyed an honoured position and are found in the *Upanishads* conversing freely with men upon the highest philosophical topics, had become virtual slaves in the joint family. Widows were treated with great cruelty, female infanticide was rife in some castes, and compulsory immolation of widows was often enforced. Theologically also, the great *Vedantic* truths that lay behind Hindu thought had been obscured by the jungle growth of superstition and corruption. The inspiration of the medieval saint-singers, while still prevalent, had begun to fade in the face of the political turmoil and widespread anarchy that followed the collapse of Mughal power. Indeed, it was one of the darkest periods in Indian history, and it seemed that Hinduism had at last exhausted its spiritual reserves, and would gradually fade away in the face of the new onslaught.

However, once again the miracle of regeneration was witnessed, and Hindu society produced a series of remarkable men who, by the sheer power of their spiritual illumination, rekindled the dying spark. In 1857, after what is commonly known as the Great Indian Mutiny, but which many now prefer to call India's First War of Independence, India lay crushed and prostrate at the feet of her foreign conquerors, broken not only in body but also in spirit. People began to lose faith in their cultural and religious heritage, and a miasma of spiritual darkness pervaded the land. And yet, within a short span of ninety years, India not only rose phoenix-like from the ashes but swept to a triumphant freedom which marked the beginning of a global process of decolonisation. This achievement can, to a large extent, be traced to a resurgence of Hinduism. This is not to deprecate in any way the role of the other communities in India's national revival, but to highlight the fact that the majority of Indians have always been Hindus, and it is Hinduism, therefore, that predominantly set the tone of a national culture in India and provided the ethos, the cultural milieu, the great backdrop, as it were, against which the drama of her history was enacted.

It was in the great movement for social reform in Hinduism that the first creative reaction to British rule manifested itself, and it was Bengal, the first province in India to feel the brunt of British conquest, that spearheaded this cultural revival. It was here that the first of a long line of great leaders of thought and action arose, a man who has often been described as the 'pathfinder' of modern India. Raja Rammohun Roy (1772-1833) was a man of unusual intellectual ability, a profound scholar of Sanskrit and Persian, as well a deep admirer of British culture. He took a leading part in starting English-medium schools in Bengal, and in 1828 founded the Brahmo Sabha, later to develop under his successor Devendranath Tagore into the Brahmo Samaj. This was the first deliberate attempt in modern India to reform Hinduism, and to cleanse it of the undesirable encrustation that had developed around it over the centuries.

The Brahmo Samaj, as well as its offshoots, the Adi Brahmo Samaj, led by Devendranath Tagore, the Brahmo Samaj of India founded by Keshub Chunder Sen in 1868, and the Sadharan Brahmo Samaj founded by some of his followers in 1878, all based themselves upon the pristine authority of the *Vedas*, and strongly attacked idol worship and undesirable social customs such as compulsory *sati,* immolation of widows upon their husband's funeral pyres. The leaders of the movement, specially Sen, were considerably influenced by the style of Christian missionaries who had become active under British rule, and many of their prayer meetings were modelled upon Christian church services.

Under the influence of the Brahmo Samaj, several such movements started in other parts of India, notably the Prarthana Samaj founded in Bombay in 1867 by the great scholars,

M.G. Ranade and R. D. Bhandarkar. These societies, while influencing mainly the English-educated fringe of society, did play an important part in bringing a new intellectual awareness into Hindu society, and encouraged educated Hindus to re-examine their religious heritage in the light of changing conditions. The same is true of the Theosophical Society which was founded by Madame Blavatsky and Colonel Olcott in New York in 1875 and gained considerable popularity in India, largely through the work of Mrs. Annie Besant. Simultaneously, the rediscovery of the ancient Indian texts by European, scholars such as Max Müller, Ferguson and Cunningham, and the work of Western archaeologists and linguists which brought to light the remarkable achievements of the Hindu past that had virtually been lost during centuries of Muslim rule, helped to give the nineteenth-century Hindu a new awareness of his rich cultural heritage and a renewed pride in his ancient religion.

All this, however, remained largely confined to the small, educated classes, awaiting a movement that would touch the heart of traditional Hinduism. This was not long in coming. A major figure in the Hindu revival was Swami Dayananda Saraswati (1824-83) who founded the Arya Samaj in 1875. Unlike the Brahmo and its offshoots, which were considerably influenced by Christianity, the Arya Samaj was militantly Hindu. Swami Dayananda passionately advocated a return to the pristine purity of *Vedic* Hinduism, and denounced with intolerant indignation the post-*Vedic* Hindu scriptures such as the *Puranas*. He also condemned idol worship and caste distinctions, advocated full equality for women, initiated a widespread educational campaign with special emphasis on female education, and launched a crusade against untouchability. Rightly described as a human dynamo, Swami Dayananda shook the structure of established Hinduism to its foundations and infused into it new blood and fresh vigour.

Numerous other reformist and educational movements in Hinduism developed in the second half of the nineteenth century. For purposes of this review, however, we shall confine ourselves to a mention of five outstanding figures who have left their indelible impress upon modern Hinduism, and whose tremendous personalities have gone a long way in shaping the contours of the Hindu mind in our own century. These are Sri Ramakrishna, Swami Vivekananda, Sri Ramana Maharshi, Sri Aurobindo and Mahatma Gandhi. Each of these men, drawn from the very heart of the Hindu tradition, reinterpreted its eternal truths in the light of his own extraordinary attainment. Between them they achieved nothing less than a comprehensive revival of the best in the Hindu tradition, and collectively represent a major force in the contemporary religious thought of the world.

Chapter Seven
Sri Ramakrishna (1836-86)

Born in a poor Brahmin family in Hooghly district, West Bengal, Gadadhar Chatterjee began showing unusual signs of religious ecstasy at a very early age. When he was nineteen, he came to Calcutta to live with his elder brother who had been appointed priest of a newly built temple at Dakshineshwar on the banks of the river Ganges. The main shrine is dedicated to the great goddess Kali, from which Kolkata derives its name, and it was as a devotee of the goddess that Sri Ramakrishna, as he came to be called, began his astounding career of spiritual discipline and attainments. Visions, trances and ecstasies crowded in upon him, and most of his time was spent in intense spiritual rhapsodies. His agonised craving to see the Divine face to face was fulfilled, and he then proceeded under various spiritual guides to experience the whole gamut of mystical relationships described in the Hindu scriptures, ranging from intense emotional raptures to the supreme beatitude of the *nirvikalpa samadhi*—contact with the all-pervasive, formless Brahman which is the highest goal of *Vedanta*. Not content with this, he proceeded to adopt the spiritual practices of Christianity and Islam, and in both cases he has recorded that they culminated in sublime spiritual experiences connected with the founders of these two great faiths.

The cumulative effect of these extraordinary phenomena was immense. By the sheer force of his spiritual attainment, Sri Ramakrishna became a beacon-light in the encircling gloom of his time. Gradually, the fame of this unlettered young priest began to spread far and wide throughout Bengal. The villager and the city dweller, the scholar and the poet, the educated and the illiterate people from all walks of life began finding their way to Dakshineshwar. Among them were some of the great luminaries from different walks of life in contemporary Bengal, men like Girish Ghose, Dr M.L. Sircar, Keshub Chunder Sen, Bijoy Krishna Goswami, Pandit Sasadhar Tarkachuramani, etc. On his own part, Sri Ramakrishna paid visits to illustrious persons like Devendranath Tagore, Iswar Chandra Vidyasagar and Bankim Chandra Chatterjee.

To all who came, Sri Ramakrishna gave the same message. He exhorted them not to waste their time squabbling over this or that creed or religion, but to seek God with a pure and dedicated heart. He reaffirmed on the basis of his own spiritual experiences that all creeds and religions led ultimately to the same goal, and he expressed his teachings in a series of homely and telling parables that made them intelligible to even the most unsophisticated villager. His sayings and the story of his life remain to this day a major source of religious inspiration.

Sri Ramakrishna showed that, far from being a dying religion as some of the newly educated intelligentsia had begun to believe, Hinduism was an inexhaustible fount of spiritual inspiration. Though he lived quietly in Dakshineshwar and seldom ventured outside the temple compound, his very presence generated a powerful current of fresh light into Hindu society. And the Bengalis, with their unusual emotional and intellectual capacities, responded eloquently to this saint. Sri Ramakrishna was, indeed, an apostle of divine realisation, one of those rare souls whose coming heralds a spiritual revolution.

Faith is the pathway to wisdom. This faith will come if one yearns in his heart for it. The most prized of God is the man of faith. To the extent that one has sinned, one should confess and earnestly beg God's forgiveness and mercy. If one does this, God will hasten to forgive and wipe away one's sins.

Chapter Eight

Swami Vivekananda (1863-1902)

Apart from his influence upon those who occasionally visited Dakshineshwar, Sri Ramakrishna attracted to his feet a group of brilliant young disciples, several of them products of the new English schools and colleges that had been recently established in Bengal. Many of these young men had lost faith in their traditional religion and were wallowing in a sea of cynicism and spiritual despair. They found in Sri Ramakrishna a source of tremendous inspiration, a man who could banish their spiritual gloom and transform their very personalities. Outstanding among these disciples was young Narendranath Dutta, later to be famous the world over as Swami Vivekananda.

One has to go all the way back to Socrates and Plato to find a parallel for the Ramakrishna-Vivekananda relationship.

Though apparently poles apart from the master, it was the student who spread his teachings far and wide until they encompassed almost the entire world. Vivekananda was a man of remarkable qualities, gifted both with a powerful physique and outstanding intellect. Just before his death, Sri Ramakrishna designated Vivekananda his spiritual heir, and after his master's passing he took upon himself the task of knitting the disciples into a dedicated band.

After wandering the entire length of India as a penniless ascetic seeking a way to propagate the ideals of his beloved master, Vivekananda heard of the Parliament of Religions that was to be held in Chicago in 1893 in connection with the World Fair. With considerable difficulty he succeeded in getting a passage to America, and after facing further hardships finally reached Chicago and enrolled himself as a delegate to the conference. His advent at the gathering had all the elements of high drama. An obscure and unknown Hindu monk, he succeeded by the very force of his personality in dominating the whole concourse which today is remembered mainly because of him. A powerful speaker with a sonorous voice and a fine command of English, Vivekananda's famous address on the first day of the Parliament created a sensation, and his subsequent speeches established him as an outstanding preacher.

In his short life of thirty-nine years, Swami Vivekananda undertook what was in effect a restatement of Hinduism in the light of the new situation that had developed during the nineteenth century. He travelled extensively in India and abroad, lecturing on the basic Vedantic principles that underlay Hinduism. He thundered against the 'Kitchen religion', the ridiculous taboos and restrictive customs that had overlaid the tremendous *Vedantic* truths. He reaffirmed not only the divinity of God but also the inherent divinity of man. A special feature of his teachings was his keen social conscience and his intense emphasis on service to the poor and the down trodden, the sick and the hungry. He often quoted the *Rig Vedic* dictum of the human life having a two fold aim—*atmano mokshartham jagat hitaya cha*—for the welfare of the world and the salvation of one's soul. One of his celebrated remarks is that it was an insult to preach religion to a man with a hungry stomach, and that the only way God could appear before the masses of India was in the form of bread. He stressed the primacy of spiritual life, preached a doctrine of inner strength and spiritual power which alone could free India from her material, intellectual and spiritual bondage, and stressed the essential unity of all religions.

Two features of Vivekananda's ministry merit special mention, as they had an abiding influence upon the revival of contemporary Hinduism. In 1897 he founded the Ramakrishna Math and Mission with headquarters at Belur near Kolkata. Although Hinduism had a long and distinguished monastic tradition going back to Adi Shankaracharya, the Ramakrishna Mission was a new order, and its approach to the problems of contemporary India was based on a modern reinterpretation of the ancient doctrines. It had a special bias towards educational and medical work, and has over the decades distinguished itself in providing relief to the victims of natural calamities such as floods and famine. In this respect, Vivekananda clearly modelled his organisation on the pattern of the Christian missionaries who had been active in India ever since the British advent. The Ramakrishna Mission today, with numerous branches in India and abroad, continues to play a significant role in spreading the gospel of Sri Ramakrishna and his great disciple.

The other feature of Swami Vivekananda's life was the contribution he made to the spread of Hindu thought abroad, specially in America. Prior to his advent, it was only a handful of Western indologists and scholars who had any real insight into the Hindu ethos, while among the general public, there flourished all sorts of grotesque impressions regarding this great religion. Vivekananda pioneered a new awareness of Hinduism in the West. His eloquent and able presentation of the essential truths that underlie Hinduism, and his broad approach of the essential unity of religions, combined to make him a unique spokesman of the eternal East to the bustling technological culture of Western society.

Vivekananda had a deep conviction that India's goal was not only to achieve her own regeneration but also to give a new spiritual impetus and light to the world. Hinduism is not a proselytising religion; therefore, Vivekananda was not seeking converts. Rather, he sought to state the basic principles of *Vedanta* and allow their inner power to work upon the minds and hearts of his listeners. Indeed, he was the torchbearer of a whole new religious movement, and the forerunner of numerous other Hindu teachers and *yogis* who continue to this day to work in the West. Thus, both in India and abroad, Vivekananda, stands as a towering figure in modern Hinduism. His advocacy of 'neo-Vedanta', as it is sometimes called, gave a new direction to traditional Hinduism, and continues to have a profound influence upon contemporary religion.

God will forgive the sinner, if he earnestly casts away his sin. Human forgiveness is the way to happiness among men. A wise man will always be ready to forgive.

Chapter Nine

Mahatma Gandhi (1869-1948)

Mahatma Gandhi is known throughout the world for his unique leadership of the Indian freedom movement, for the concepts of *satya* and *ahimsa* (truth and non-violence) which were the cornerstones of his political philosophy, and for the manner in which he was able to shake the foundations of the great British Empire. Indeed, the Indian freedom movement marked the end of the colonial era that had dominated the world scene for the preceding three centuries, and India's independence in 1947 heralded the emergence into freedom of dozens of other nations that had for long been the victims of colonial subjugation. Mahatma Gandhi is today revered in India as the Father of the Nation, and remains a source of not only inspiration in India but wherever man is still struggling for freedom.

It is useful to remember, however, that Gandhi's approach to politics was broadly based on Hindu principles. He was himself a devout Hindu, and will go down in history as one of the greatest social reformers that Hinduism has produced. In a way he combined the two streams of thought—radical and moderate—in the freedom movement. While accepting the radicals' goal of *Purna Swaraj* or complete independence, he also breathed new life into the reform movements that the moderate leaders had espoused. Gandhi's main contribution to Hinduism was the manner in which he took up the problem of untouchables, whose ill-treatment had been one of the most disgraceful features of Hindu society. By renaming them as Harijans, or children of god, he made a symbolic gesture of atonement, and thereafter, he pursued a policy of living in Harijan colonies wherever he went, personally cleaning latrines and giving depressed classes a sense of self-esteem and involvement in the mainstream of Hindu society. The special reservations in legislatures, services and educational institutions are a direct result of Gandhi's influence and the remarkable contribution of Dr B.R. Ambedkar, the Harijan leader.

Another major contribution made by Gandhi was the involvement of women in large numbers in the freedom movement, and the stress he laid upon their social emancipation.

His 'Constructive Programme', which included the propagation of handicrafts and cottage industries, also had an egalitarian effect upon Hindu society. All his prayer meetings began with *Ram Dhun,* chanting of the Lord's Name, and for his concept of the perfect government he went back to the *Rama Rajya,* the ideal rule in the ancient days of Sri Rama. He wrote a commentary on the *Bhagavad Gita* which he looked upon as a perennial source of inspiration. He encouraged the worship of the cow, not so much on religious grounds but as a symbol of the beneficent symbiosis between human and animal existence.

Gandhi's concept of 'truth' is deeply based on the Hindu tradition. The famous words of the *Mundaka Upanishad—satyam eva jayate* (truth alone triumphs)—constituted his motto. This was adopted as India's national motto after independence. His insistence on *ahimsa* (non-violence) also had its roots in one aspect of Hinduism, although this was stressed more in the Buddhist and Jain traditions. His autobiography, *My Experiments with Truth,* is a remarkable document, and shows Gandhi's deep commitment to the fundamental ideals of Hinduism. While he never claimed to be a religious leader and always displayed the utmost humility in such matters, he was categorical in his assertion that for him religion had primacy over all other aspects, and that it was absurd to hold that politics had nothing to do with religion. He stressed the Hindu concept of the essential unity and harmony of all religions, and his prayer meetings would include readings from other religious scriptures in addition to those from Hinduism. He was greatly influenced by the saint-singers of medieval India, specially Kabir and Mirabai, and shared their and simple approach to religion of the masses.

During his three decades of political pre-eminence in India, Gandhi's contribution to the regeneration of Hinduism and the reform of Hindu society was monumental. He must, therefore, be ranked not only as a unique political leader but also as one of the main formative influences in modern Hinduism, a man who left the indelible impress of his personality not only upon his country but upon his religion as well.

In addition to these five outstanding personalities of modern Hinduism, numerous other major figures on the contemporary Hindu scene have made their contribution to the regeneration and re-interpretation of Hinduism in our own century. Most of them have founded their own societies and religious organisations. These include such persons as Yogananda Paramahansa who preached in America and founded the Yogoda Society; Swami Nikhilananda and Swami Prabhavananda of the Ramakrishna Mission in the USA; Swami Sivananda of

Rishikesh who founded the Divine Life Society; Swami Bhaktivedanta Prabhupada, whose Krishna Consciousness movement has made such a mark in the West, and Sri Krishna Prem, an Englishman who has written glowing commentaries on the *Bhagavad Gita* and the *Katha Upanishad* and who, along with his *guru* Yashoda Mai, founded a Krishna temple near Almora in the Himalayas.

Look upon all the living beings as your bosom friends, for in all of them there resides one soul. All are but a part of that Universal Soul. A person who believes that all are his soul-mates and loves them all alike never feels lonely.

Chapter Ten
Sri Aurobindo (1872-1950)

Born on 15 August 1872 in Calcutta, Aurobindo Ghosh was sent to school in England at the age of seven. There, first at the Manchester Grammar School, then at St. Paul's in London and finally at King's College, Cambridge, he underwent a full educational career covering fourteen years during which he passed the classics tripos in the first division and won college prizes for English and literary ability. He returned to India in 1893 at the age of twenty-one, and entered Baroda State Service as Professor of English, then Vice-Principal and later Principal of Baroda College.

Aurobindo was gifted with a brilliant mind and a deep psychic power. While in England he read the writings on the Irish Sinn Fein movement and the Italian Risorgimento. This filled him with a fervent sense of patriotism, and back home he began taking a keen interest in the freedom movement, still in its infancy.

In 1885 an Englishman, Alan Octavian Hume, founded the Indian National Congress, and soon there developed two clear trends of thinking in this great organisation, the 'moderates' who aimed at gradual transfer of power, and the 'extremists' whose ideal was full freedom at once. Sri Aurobindo soon became a leader of the extremists along with Lokmanya B.G. Tilak, and in 1905, when the British pushed through the highly controversial partition of Bengal, he quit his Baroda job and plunged into the national movement.

For five years, from 1905 to 1910, Aurobindo shone like a meteor on the political firmament. His brilliant editorials in the *Bande Mataram* and *Karmayogin,* patriotic journals he edited, are among the most outstanding of political writings in the English. His political philosophy was deeply rooted in the Hindu tradition of mother-worship, particularly pronounced in Bengal. Drawing his inspiration from the famous Bengali novel *Ananda Math* by Bankim Chandra Chatterjee, written half a century earlier, and in particular from the poem 'Bande Mataram' (Hail to Thee, Mother) contained therein, Aurobindo developed a comprehensive political philosophy. The key concept was the divinity of the motherland, which he idealised as the goddess Bhavani Bharati, and flowing from that the concept of nationalism not simply as a political credo but as a spiritual imperative. The spiritual nationalism, expounded by him, had an electrifying effect upon the youth of Bengal and other parts of India at that crucial juncture; and, though the movement did not meet with immediate success, it brought about for the first time a mass involvement, and left an indelible impress upon the Indian freedom movement.

While at Baroda Sri Aurobindo had begun following some yogic practices, and during the Bengal agitation he was arrested in the celebrated Alipur Bomb Conspiracy Case and kept in jail for over a year. It was during this enforced solitude that the spiritual trend in his psyche gained predominance; and, though after his acquittal he continued for some time with political activities, he realised that his real life-work lay elsewhere. In 1910, on a sudden inner impulse, he left Bengal for the French possession of Chandernagore, and from there moved on to the other French possession of Pondicherry where he lived for forty years until his death in 1950. In the course of his four decades at Pondicherry, Sri Aurobindo developed one of the most comprehensive and original systems of thought in modern times. He based himself upon the Hindu tradition, but gave creative interpretations to the ancient texts including the *Vedas* and the *Upanishads*. His masterly work, *Essays on the Gita,* is perhaps the most outstanding of the many commentaries that have been written upon this sacred text since Shankaracharya, while his chief literary work, *The Life Divine,* the massive epic poem, *Savitri,* and numerous other works stand as a testimony to his gigantic intellect and deep intuition.

If his political philosophy can be called spiritual nationalism, Sri Aurobindo's general philosophy can well be called spiritual evolution. He rejects the traditional Hindu concept of individual salvation, and stresses those aspects of the Hindu tradition that speak of raising the collective consciousness of the race. The key concept in his thought is that of spiritual evolution. According to Sri Aurobindo, man is the result of aeons of evolution from unicellular organisms up through mineral, vegetable and animal forms. However, he is by no means the end-product of evolution. Sri Aurobindo postulates a further evolutionary thrust from man with his mental faculties to superman with supramental faculties. Indeed, he holds that it is only with the next quantum leap in the evolutionary adventure that mankind will break out of its present impasse and fulfil its spiritual destiny.

Sri Aurobindo wrote at great length with regard to this leap, and presented for its fulfilment his own path which he called 'Integral Yoga' because it seeks to draw together the strands of the four traditional *yogas* into a single, multi-faceted spiritual endeavour. Sri Aurobindo's goal was not individual salvation, not even racial salvation, it was nothing less than a fundamental change in the texture of terrestrial consciousness itself, the creation of 'a new heaven and a new earth'. Often described as the pioneer of the supramental, Sri Aurobindo's 'Integral Yoga', worked out with the active collaboration of his companion, Madame Alfassa, known as the Mother, has three broad movements: first, a complete and integral surrender to the divine; second, a raising of the human consciousness to the supramental level; and, third, a return to earth after absorbing the power and light of the supramental so that its influence can be directly brought to bear upon terrestrial life. This stress on evolution, though based essentially upon Hindu texts, marks a new development in contemporary Hinduism which has still not fully unfolded itself.

*G*iving with cheerfulness is the way to security and happiness. Giving is superior to receiving since the giver acquires a friend and protects himself from enemies. The wise man will always share with others.

Chapter Eleven

Sri Ramana Maharshi (1879-1950)

If Sri Ramakrishna was a *bhakta* par excellence and Swami Vivekananda a *karma-yogi,* Sri Ramana was in the great Hindu tradition the *Jnana-yogi.* Belonging to a middle-class Brahmin family of Tamil Nadu, Ramana, at the ago of seventeen, had a series of powerful spiritual experiences that culminated in his taking up permanent residence at the holy Arunachala Hill with the town of Tiruvannamalai at its foot. Here he gradually started attracting a group of devotees, and lived for the rest of his life as a revered saint, or *maharshi,* recognised by all as a powerful figure on the spiritual firmament.

Sri Ramana's teachings expound the *Vedantic* path of self-knowledge, and his original works as well as commentaries upon the Hindu classics all flow from the process of self-enquiry. The question 'Who am I?' is to be found in most religious traditions, because the quest for self-knowledge is at the heart of every spiritual endeavour. But Sri Ramana made this the cornerstone of his whole philosophy. To every question he would respond by asking a counter-question. 'Who is it that asks?' Thus when the body, the senses, the mind are all negated, the real 'I' begins to shine forth in all its glory.

This process of spiritual introspection was presented by Sri Ramana with great clarity, and he also taught a process of *pranayama* or breath control that would assist the seeker to still the modifications of the mind and focus the psychic energy upon asking that single question, 'Who am I?' He likened this to the flaming brand that is used to light a great fire; it not only sets the entire material ablaze but also consumes itself in the process. Thus Sri Ramana taught that the question 'Who am I?', if properly and persistently asked, has the capacity to destroy all delusion and ultimately itself disappear with the dawn of spiritual realisation.

Unlike Vivekananda, Sri Ramana never concerned himself with social service or reform movements. He seldom ventured outside his abode at Arunachalam, and yet such was his spiritual presence that he commanded veneration from all sides. The thousands who trekked to see him were often content to do just that, because in the Hindu tradition even the sight of a holy person—*darshana*—has its own spiritual merit. Sri Ramana had an extraordinary presence. Quite unconcerned with outer events, he was as one permanently centred in the Brahman, and his words came not from intellectual brilliance but from a perfect inner assurance. Like Sri Ramakrishna before him, he was a living proof of the spiritual power of Hinduism. It said that the night he passed away after undergoing a long and painful ailment with no sign of suffering or complaint, a bright comet moved across the sky and shone for a while in splendour above Arunachalam before disappearing behind the holy mountain.

This list is by no means exhaustive, but is enough to show that Hinduism is in one of its important phases of creative resurgence. The rise of science and technology, on the one hand, and of communism with its atheistic implications, in the other, is a profound challenge to established religions throughout the world. To survive, a mere reiteration of old orthodoxies is not enough. What is required is a reinterpretation of ancient truths in the light of contemporary compulsions, and this Hinduism has done time and again in its long and eventful history.

True happiness comes not from external things, but through attachment to things spiritual. It is an inner joy which nothing outside can destroy. It comes from God and is a reward for goodness. Only the wise have real happiness.

Chapter Twelve
The Future

Mankind faces a complex dilemma at this stage of its evolution. Science and technology, if wisely used, have given him for the first time the capacity to abolish deprivation and poverty, illiteracy and disease, unemployment and inequality from the face of the earth. On the other hand, the same science has also given him the power to destroy not only the human race but perhaps all life. There is a great churning of the collective consciousness of humanity, and a tremendous urge for new certitudes to take the place of the old bulwarks that are collapsing. In such a situation, all religions face a fundamental challenge. Hinduism, with its tremendous capacity for regeneration and reinterpretation, should not have anything to fear. Indeed, India, with its rich and varied religious heritage as well as the most distinguished pool of scientific talent in the developing world, should be able to give the right lead to humanity at this crucial juncture.

The contribution of Hinduism, in the past, to world civilisation has been many-faceted. It covers, to mention just a few fields, mathematics (the discovery of zero or *shoonya* which was the prerequisite for any advance in this highly abstract science); medicine (through *Ayurveda,* one of the most ancient and integrated systems of medicine known to man); architecture (which produced such wonders as the rock-cut caves of Ellora and the great temple cities of South India); dance (with the Bharatanatyam and other classical dance forms based upon Bharata's great treatise, the *Natya Shastra*); music (both in the Carnatic tradition and the Hindustani mode which has had such an impact in recent years upon the West); psychology (through *yoga,* which represents the most profound enquiry into the mysteries of the human mind and psyche yet developed by man); linguistics and literature (through the vehicle of Sanskrit, unparalleled in its power and majesty, and other great languages including Tamil); and of course, philosophy (from the luminous utterance of the *Upanishads* to Swami Vivekananda and Sri Aurobindo in this century). In these and other fields too numerous to catalogue, the Hindu mind has contributed to the corpus of human knowledge and attainment in a manner of which few religions can boast.

Hinduism retains an inner dynamism and presents certain key concepts that are particularly relevant in this nuclear age, not only for Hindus but also for the entire human race. The five seminal ideas that follow have been chosen for the width of their outlook that transcends religious and denominational barriers, and gives them universal relevance.

The Unity of Mankind

Every country has developed a love for its own nationhood, but there are few that have had the capacity to rise above the imposing mansion of nationalism and conceptualise the unity of the entire human race. It has been the Hindu genius that, although it has accepted and reiterated nationalism in the modern sense, particularly after the great renaissance in the nineteenth century, its best minds have always held up the concept of mankind as a single family, *vasudhaiva kutumbakam,* as the *Rig Veda* has it. The relevance of this to the present human predicament is obvious. Science and technology have now converted what was once only a vision in the minds of seers into a concrete reality. Time and space are shrinking before our eyes, and the extraordinary photograph of earth taken from the moon shows our planet, as it really is, a tiny spaceship hurtling through the endless vastnesses of space, so beautiful and yet so fragile. The essential unity of the race that inhabits this planet, based upon the fact of 'humanness' itself, is thus a concept that is growing increasingly relevant as this century draws to its close and mankind struggles desperately to survive its own technological ingenuity.

The Harmony of Religions

The second great concept that Hinduism has developed through the ages is that of the harmony of religions. The yearning of the human for the divine, which is at the heart of the religious quest, has in practice often been translated into hideous strife between the followers of different religions, each convinced of its own righteousness and of cruel persecution within various religions themselves. The Hindu ethos, however, has always accepted different paths to the divine—*ekam sad viprah bahuda vadanti* (Truth is one, the wise call it by many names) as the *Rig Veda* has it. Apart from Hinduism, which has always been the predominant religion of India, there are millions of Muslims, Buddhists, Jains, Sikhs, Parsis, Christians (of several denominations) and Jews who have lived peacefully in this country for centuries. There are also famous shrines and pilgrimage-centres sacred to all these religions.

The unique synthesis achieved in Kashmir between the Shaiva tradition and the Sufi influx, resulting in the *rishi* cult equally sacred to Hindus and Muslims, is only one of the more dramatic manifestations of the Hindu tradition of religious harmony. Tolerating another religion is at best a negative approach, but accepting all religions positively and gladly is a peculiarly Hindu contribution. Its message of the harmony of religions, of the essential unity of mystical experiences, of accepting the divine as so opulent and all-embracing that any effort to move towards it is to be welcomed regardless of its style or idiom, is thus extremely relevant in the modern age.

The Divinity of the Individual

Flowing from the concept of the unity of mankind and the harmony of religions is the third aspect of the Hindu message which reiterates the divinity and dignity of the individual. It is true that Hindu society often appears to be so highly hierarchical and stratified and places so much emphasis upon social duty and status that individual freedom seems to be at a discount. However, it must be remembered that parallel to and, ultimately, overriding these social stratifications runs the basic concept of the divinity of the human individual. Every person born into the human race, regardless of sex or religion, colour or caste, language or geographical location partakes of the essential mystery of divine potential. Every Atman, in the Hindu view, contains the seeds of spiritual growth and ultimate realisation.

Howsoever diverse the circumstances, howsoever hostile the environment, Hinduism believes that there is within the human psyche the unquenchable spark of divinity that can, sooner or later, be fanned into the blazing fire of spiritual realisation. This concept endows every individual with a dignity that immediately places him, in essence, above and beyond social customs and traditions. Today, when human dignity is at a discount with various collectivities imposing their domination over the individual in a hundred different ways, this aspect of Hinduism's message is of no mean significance. It provides the counterpoint to the concept of human unity, reasserting the unique significance of each individual while stressing the unity of the entire race.

The Quality of Creative Synthesis

The fourth facet of the Hindu ethos flows from its unusual synthesising and syncretising capacity. Against the rigid dichotomy between action in the world and withdrawn meditation, it places the great ideal of the *Gita,* wherein the way of *karma* (action) and the way of *jnana* (knowledge) are fused in the crucible of dedication to the divine; against the cruel dichotomy between matter and energy (which has only recently been breached in the West by Einstein and his successors), the Indian mind has postulated the essential oneness behind all existence—*isha vasyamidam sarvam yat kincha jagatyam jagat*—as the *Isha Upanishad* has it, the same energy pulsating in the heart of the atom as in the depths of the farthest galaxy; against the dogmatic confrontation between science and religion, there is the vision of both these great disciplines as two different approaches towards essentially the same truth, one reaching outwards into the very structure of the cosmos and the other inwards into the very essence of the human psyche. This capacity to balance, to harmonise disparate concepts and apparently contradictory movements, has been the hallmark of the greatest Hindu minds, and carries within it the ideological seeds of a world civilisation in the future which, ideally, would weld together the best traditions of national cultures into a glowing and harmonious synthesis.

Cosmic Values

Finally, in the context of our newly achieved capacity to break away from the confines of this planet and begin a tentative advance into the vastnesses of outer space, Hinduism has provided a scheme of cosmic values which are startling in their contemporary relevance. The concept of vast aeons of time through which the world passes (four ages or *yugas* totalling 4.32 billion years, each adding up to only a single day of Brahma) more closely approximates to the age of this earth than any other scheme of classical calculation. The concept of millions upon millions of galaxies, *koti koti brahmanda,* once considered to be merely an absurd flight of fancy, is now beginning to come alive as the boundless universe unfolds itself before our startled gaze. The vision of the cosmic dance of Shiva, where millions of galaxies spring into being every moment and millions are extinguished in the unending cycle of eternity, is only now beginning to reflect the knowledge that we are receiving from our initial probings into the universe around us.

And yet, within this incomprehensible vastness, perhaps because of it, remains the eternal mystery of the human personality. Among billions of galaxies in the universe, one is ours; among billions of stars in this galaxy one is ours; among billions of human beings in this solar system one of them is ourselves, but such is the grandeur and mystery of the Atman that it can move towards a comprehension of the unutterable mystery of existence. We, who are children of the past and the future, of earth and heaven, of light and darkness, of the human and the divine, at once evanescent and eternal, of the world and beyond it, within time and in eternity, yet have the capacity to comprehend our condition, to rise above our terrestrial limitations, and finally, to transcend the throbbing abyss of space and time itself. This, in essence, is the message of Hinduism.

Words of Wisdom

One becomes what one does. The doer of good deeds will become good and the doer of evil deeds will become evil. Action, the doing of the good, is superior to renunciation. Thus, at all times, one should be doing good.

The soul destroys the earthly body in order to make for itself a new and more beautiful body. The wise man will become immortal. Death is the taking off of the robe of life to put on the robe of immortality. The good and just shall live forever.

Love and respect must reign in the home. This is commended because every member of the household is a soul and as a soul he is worthy of love and respect. Faithfulness must mark the relationship of husband and wife.

The highest law of the home is fidelity among its members. The wife should be faithful, the children obedient, and the father understanding and industrious. Thus will develop the perfect home.

Wrath breeds confusion. One who would be measter of himself and of all situations must avoid wrath. The ideal is to live free from hate and anger.

Causing injury to any creature is wrong. The wise man will seek always to avoid strife and will dwell in peace. The ideal for life here on earth is peace, not war. No one should seek to extend his power through war.

Anger produces confusion. He who would be clear and unconfused must avoid becoming angry.

He who is evil cannot hope to attain eternal happiness. Heaven punishes the evil. All pain and suffering comes from evil-doing.

*H*atred breeds confusion.
Clear thinking and careful action can come only when the heart is free from hatred.

The laws of God are eternal, lofty, and deep. The man who is obedient to them will be happy and, after death, will experience joy unsurpassable.

*M*an is the highest of animals. He is an animal with an immortal soul which cannot be hurt by the world. There is nothing nobler than humanity.

The one who hurts pious men falls victim to his own designs. This is divine justice.

*T*he Lord is the lover of all beings, but He especially loves those who keep His laws and are devoted to Him. One can best worship the Lord through love.

Those who do not meditate can have neither steadiness nor peace. The great and the wise meditate constantly on the divine. This is the source of strength and the way to knowledge of the Supreme One.

*O*ne should work constantly and seek after wealth. But, if one gains wealth, one should share it with those in need. Beware lest wealth shut the door one the good life. Riches are but means to doing good and should not become the goal of life.

No enemies can overcome the believer. He trusts in God, knowing that God will guide him through all troubles. If one would find happiness and security, one must seek for peace. The peaceful mind will become established in wisdom. God is a god of peace and desires peace for all people.